Under a Prairie Moon

by
Susie Niedermeyer

BLUE LIGHT PRESS ◆ 1ST WORLD PUBLISHING

1ˢᵗ WORLD
PUBLISHING

SAN FRANCISCO ◆ FAIRFIELD ◆ DELHI

Winner of the 2007 Blue Light Book Award

UNDER A PRAIRIE MOON

Copyright ©2009 by Susie Niedermeyer

1ST WORLD LIBRARY
106 South Court Street
Fairfield, Iowa 52556
www.1stworldpublishing.com

BLUE LIGHT PRESS
1563 45th Avenue
San Francisco, California, 94122

AUTHOR PHOTO
Diana Krystofiak

BOOK AND COVER DESIGN
Melanie Gendron
www.melaniegendron.com

COVER ART
Bonnie Jaye

FIRST EDITION

LCCN: 2009929647

ISBN: 978-1-4218-9099-9

For My Mother,
Elinor Frances MacLeod

ACKNOWLEDGEMENTS

The author extends grateful acknowledgement to the following publications where her poems first appeared.

"Passamezzo" (*Lyric Iowa* and *Leaves by Night, Flowers by Day*)
"Concealed Destiny" (*The MacGuffin*)
"Polishing the Quiet" (*Iowa Sierran* and *The Dryland Fish: An Anthology of Contemporary Iowa Poets*)
"The Rats" (*Hard Row to Hoe*)
"The Dancers" (*Sweet Annie*)
"Owl at Dusk" (*Sweet Annie*)
"Spring Rain" (*Sweet Annie*)
"Under Glass" (*Sweet Annie*)
"Sunflowers" (*Sweet Annie*)

"Playing Rachmaninoff" received Honorable Mention in the Ohio Poetry Association's Winter Solstice Contest, 2003.

"Diana" received second place in the National Federation of State Poetry Societies, Inc., Forty-third Annual Contest, 2002.

I would like to extend my gratitude to the following people and organizations for their support and encouragement: Diane Frank, The Monday Night Poets, Bryan Aubrey, and Rustin Larson.

—S.N.

CONTENTS

THE BARN

Under the late gestation moon
the barn lies heavy in the half light,
its mouth an open byway
to an endless menagerie,
its breath of cindered honey.

Grey timbers bared to arctic blasts,
windows rattle in their sills.
Like yesterday's dream
it touches its inhabitants gently,
encompassing the sibilant fury of a feral cat,
a coterie of pigeons,
and the dignity of its many dead:
tufted mouse, fetal sparrow, setting hen.

A worn outpost near extinction,
it has seen countless summer days,
swallows soaring like high-wire fliers,
the sun pouring slow pools of gold
through its ribs, transforming
hayloft into holy sanctum,
dust motes drifting like veils of mist.

GEESE

Above Hickory Hills pond
delirious geese melt out of the sky
speaking in tongues.
Their jabber wavers
like grass in the wind
and their erratic vee
wobbles its circumspect calligraphy,
crossing the moon.

Kohl-eyed, bodies oiled
smooth by the wind,
speak of air
the color of the sea
and myriad miles of stars.
The dry hiss of wings
pumps night-blood—
they listen with their bones.

My heart thuds when I hear
those cries come shimmering
out of their mouths,
dissonant chords echoing
in the blue. Still as a fish
I sit alone, listening,
on a quiet quilt of loam.

THE DANCERS

The wind lifts the arms
of long needled pines,
impels them to dance
in the ever widening
circles of twilight.
For the longest and sweetest time
the sun slips
cloud by cloud
over the pond and into the trees.

Beyond the rushes
light coalesces into form.
Dancers rise, half in dream,
move apart, then gently turning
lean down close, their radiance merging
before dark and feathered wings
lift one, then another
to hover, still as dragonflies
or lovers with all the time in the world.

Here by this pond
I feel a power, an exultation
in the presence of the wind,
the light and the fire
and the dull throb under my ribs
that wants to rise golden
into my throat and beyond,
as I walk the green grass
to water's edge.

OWL AT DUSK

The sky at dusk is liquid
in the blue-grey of the pond.
Slowly it leans down
enveloping the land
with veils of indigo,
uncurling the tendrils
of the mind. Cool air,
flow of silk on skin.

An owl waits on the barn roof,
all darkness and hunger,
ready to slip onto the currents of the night.
When dawn comes he returns
with bloodied beak and talons.

He does not mourn the shattered lives,
or that his days are few.
At milking time I've seen him
on a rafter, winking.

POLISHING THE QUIET

My roots reach deep into Iowa soil
as I walk this afternoon, drinking in
the roadside slash of blowing grasses,
the muddy fields, grey skies. In my blood
I feel the sentient force of tiny seeds,
embryos flung like light under winter
houses of the zodiac, waiting in the
wet kiss of the soil that surrounds them.

Three vultures float overhead, poised
on air and crying their darkness, their hisses
bright with blood as they scissor down
to feed on a hunter's refuse, slate eyes blank
as the shadow of an empty mirror.
Already too bloated to rise
they flap at dark turkeys
in a burst of wingfire and vanish.

In the shadows of late afternoon
I hold small stones in my hand.
The sky melts pink on the dark tongue
of the pond and here, alone, I want to know
unseen things. I want to close my eyes
and give my limbs to the tender earth
and beading rain, to dance
a slow tango, adoring the world.

CONCEALED DESTINY

In the dark barn I stand
with my big bay doe, full in kid.
Her fatal flaw, one frozen teat
that hangs hard and dark.
Awaiting their birth
she doesn't know
she'll never feed them.

Heavy, the earth pulling her down,
she is inward, restless,
rolling her eyes.
A translucent bubble appears,
then disappears, breaks,
as she struggles to her feet.
Her waters soak into yellow straw.

Down again, a white hoof appears.
Brown flanks wet and heaving
she bellows into her pain
that is suddenly over.
A tiny goat kid is born,
and another,
and bounteous mother
yet one more.

Not yet knowing
her body will betray her,
she whispers, licking them dry.
But when they finally
stand braced on newborn legs
and weave to her side
as if gravity were somehow
a fickle partner in the dance,
I interfere, knowing I have no choice.

Udder hard, pink, and full
I take from her good teat
the last life she has to give.
In her milky-blue essence
lies her spirit, her fear
of the coyotes that run in the dark
and her love of lilies, kale
and blackberry leaves.

Lying down now,
watching me with her young,
she is not yet deceived.
I feed them, then leave them
with her for the night,
knowing by morning she'll
understand my treachery
and her fate.

THE COYOTES

It was birthing time and the barn rose
luminous under an eggshell moon.
In the half light I could see them
streaming by and hear the laughing
yip and howl of them.

Then silence, but for the skitter
of a rat in the manger
and the heavy night sighs
of the does.

I told myself the fence is sound,
mice and fawns are plenty,
but my fear that night was
not of flesh and blood
but the oldest fear,
the myriad forms
of shadowed
darkness.

RECALLING A NIGHT IN AUGUST

When I first entered the old farmhouse
I knew it as a memory, a second skin.
I could have walked it blind,
knew it like the body of a lover.

Alone on the porch, cicadas buzzing,
I am sending my own eerie love calls
through time to reclaim the night that
pale green meteors flared like quail.
We hover on the lawn
with the night scent of nicotiana,
blankets spread and music flooding out
into phantom crops of jimson and clover.

Talk takes the shapes of our dreams
and laughter echoes like distant thunder
until it's time to say goodbye
(headlights piercing dust, like fog)
and retreat to the intimate circuitry
of our own silence.

Alone in my room I become night's child
and pull down an imaginary shade.
Frugal stars winking their illusion
are nested like trilobites in onyx.
We watch each other and I become
weightless, unlocalized, a quasar
pulsed with veins of gold.

To the stars I say,
Come, touch me,
I too am falling fire.

THE LETTER

Since we parted you have lived
in that stillness where thought begins,
though I've misplaced the evidence.
Olive skin, suede brogans,
dark curls, but what of a face?
The photos in my mind are tea-stained
and torn. Echoes I hear, but not a voice.
But suddenly you're back in an envelope,
among the bank statements and catalogs,
white as gesso and brave as a kiss
that blows away the years.
Your words stir me like a stranger imposing
a waltz and I tumble out of the nest
all feathers and blur, trying to reconnect
my silence to the face I half see
in the dark night falling.
You have opened a window
in my winter house of secrets
and the wind's insistent whisper blows back
the velvet curtains, raising dust,
and gusts through the untended garden,
ruffling the fur of an ancient tabby
and spilling the red petals of a rose.
The difference is not in the taste of the sun on my lips
or the opalescing brightness
reflected endlessly between earth and sky,
but how a word on a page opens me beyond words,
beyond the faintest heartbeat.

CODA

— How precarious the glue of our communion.
Lucia Perillo

The music lifts my heavy body by the spine
and my wrists over the piano keys
as I silently play the invisible.
Rewinding and moaning with the scratches,
I feel the weight of the violinist's arm,
the bite of rosin, their perfect communion.
All day I am followed by the color of rain
remembering . . .

how on the night of my best friend's 13th birthday
I lifted a crystal glass in toast,
my teeth finding the fine, thin rim.
When it shattered in the startle of photoflash,
I spit pink shards into damask
and blushing, stammered that it must have been
already cracked.

A year later she waded into the river
and discovered midway in her heavy limbs,
no end to the water.
The same Elgar Chanson de Matin
played as her ashes were strewn
onto a carpet of ginger-lilies in the Iowa woods.

Music, beginnings, endings, births, deaths,
things run down or run their course,
a body simply done with living;
it's the same celebration.

I remember too, how on the last night
of my grandmother's life
my sister bends over the bed,
her straight blond hair fallen forward
hiding their faces. We dance
a languid tango in the kitchen
and grandma's map of wrinkles folds
into a smile.

A silver needle of moonlight
falls through the trees,
weaving tangles into her hair.
For her we're playing our music now,
my sister's Trio Colore.
Her breath comes deep and rasping,
and though I've never heard the sound before,
I know its name.

She surfaces, says she's fine.
I know it's true and not true.
Most things are that way now.

Interior Landscape

Two months longing, of endless winter
afternoons. Two months insomnia,
watching the twisting smoke of incense,
unbroken in cold rooms. Sepia shadows
crease the wall; the mirror reflects
rivers of birds. Two months
rain never leaves my blood.
Words recalled become sacred,
collect in the back of my throat.

Some nights I dream of the naked forest
under stars—black limbs
reaching for the sky. I discover
you within me in new places,
my skin alive, each hair.
I feel winged, transparent.

Memory hauls my belongings
out into the rain,
moving slowly, weighed down
by moments caught in her skein,
in the gauzy swirl of her skirts.
Like pictures, I sort through them,
recalling, dissolving, collecting.
When you finally appear
your image comes slowly,
like a Polaroid.
I only half believe it.

THE ARGUMENT

Sitting on the porch swing
this cool summer's night,
the white moon leans close,
cracked by a twig.
I recall words
I do not care to admit,
abstract now, forgettable
in the seductive,
liquid black of night.

You approach on the chalky
gravel road edged by dark walls
of corn, a deep light in the silence
above the quiet breathing
of the land. From the red maple
an owl drops, a tiny cry silenced,
and I feel my heart pound—
a small death,
the slamming of a door.

We have hours ahead
through dark and greener dark
as the heart's fever burns
before the calm of first light,
forgiveness and the laying out
of tea and bread.

November Repast

I hate the cold gravel roads
that crisscross the quadrants of my day.
As I drive I shriek at the cows
clumped like raisins in lumpy oatmeal fields,
the green scraped off the landscape
like uneaten spinach off a plate.

How angry I've been at the predator wind
that yanks at my scarf
and the leaves that levitate in doorways
and ghost across the highway.
I'm collecting Japanese beetles in jars,
the ones that bite my neck
and fall from the ceiling into my tea.

Inside the weather's just as bad—futile acts
of contrition, guilt thick as grits.
You hole up like a drowsy snake
in front of your computer, and we send emails
through a 1910 plaster wall, reconfiguring
the parameters of a marriage.

I feel heavy as a rotting persimmon,
bleeding vital juices onto a plate.
I don't know how to live any life
other than this, here in frigid Iowa.
The chill clings to me like shrink wrap
and my limbs are stiff as celery.
Can't we just go home?

NIGHT WITH COWS

Cows drift from their sheds at dusk,
udders brushing the heads of tall grasses,
ready for love and feasting. Paths glow
like runways, float in moonlight.

We follow a map of scents, carry longing
in trembling hands. Invisible,
it throws shadow-rivers, stampedes
into liquid grasses, and burrows into the flesh
of a field, splashed with crows.

The first stars start to burn
through green rain and the silver slip of minnows.
Time dissolves into touch that spreads
like a constellation. Your tongue
slides down my back, paints a seam of phosphor.

Where are you when your body's remembering?
Where, when your hand lies forgotten
along my ribs and you're terracing
the cerulean deltas of sleep?
Love is thin fire under the skin,
ears roaring.

We rise, leaving our impress in ferns,
breath hot in their lace and curl. Blinking
at the moon, you smooth the map of your skin.
The cows in the distance float like barges.

Two-Year Storm

A quiet thought comes
now and again, like the lone pheasant
who visits the field near the house,
a perfect life stepping carefully
over old stalks of corn,
foraging like a god.
No one can truly know another.

When the last light has seeped down
behind the web of trees,
the last tumbled canyons of cropland
faded to darkness, I remember how at first,
unafraid, you heard in me the answer
to your wild dreams. Now you are deaf
to all but the sibilant litany of my fears.

For some time it seemed
each of us walked in a cloud,
dissolving in our own white exile.
But here you are, the lamplight
flickering in your pupils, and I see
the tattered book of our story
still open, as I peer over your shoulder
and hear the hiss of desire
in the singing of locusts in the trees.

For the moment I hold the cool hands
of reticence and remorse.
Life seems to pass, illusory milestones
dwindling into the horizon,
yet remains with its blackbird eyes,
feet skittering among the elephant ferns.
Not a feather out of place, anywhere.

ADVENT OF AUTUMN

All at once, from the mature green everywhere,
a knowing has come. Soft as wine
on a woman's breath
it seeped in under the door,
climbed in the window like a thief.
Gone are the warm transparent afternoons,
the fruits and thousand fragrances.
Let me savor the cool breeze,
the shadows of clouds, and remember
how the trees reached for the apricot sky
like the lines on the palm of your hand.

From all our moments something
must remain, though my eyes see
only the empty seat beside me.
You are intangible now,
yet in our season breathed in gladly
like the fragrant, damp earth.

Ah, but it's warm inside, the fire burns bright.
Why should I grieve when your presence
falls ever so gently over me, now and then,
and weighs no more than a feather.
So come inside, bring the last pink rose,
and we will share the silence.

Earth's Lament

I'm losing her.
Though she still rakes my paths
and lines them with needles of pine,
reaps the lambs quarter and nettles
I grow for her bones,
energy is coalescing around her heart
and she's withdrawing.

Even as we share the velvet night
she is pulling away. I love her
as if she'll return, as if together
we'd invented moonlight.
Her tears fall upon me.

Though she still gathers up the bones
of winter's long white reign,
runs her fingers through my fertile loam
and looks deep into the liquid dark of my eye,
I know in time she will leave me.

Over my waters she scatters
all she's lost . . . every broken vow
as above us the blackbirds sign their names
in the sky.   She promises return
but I know she's saying goodbye.

LINE OF SIGHT

Maybe it's the time of year again.
The sky's still light at seven,

the breath of music you almost recognize
when someone opens a door,

the barest touch of a finger on your sleeve
reminds you she's still out there somewhere.

You find yourself feeling
that pull of the heart

the way an old jockey suddenly
wants to toss his silken cap to the crowd

when he smells a rose
or sees a certain configuration

of buildings as he rounds a corner.
Sometimes it is something

as impossibly blue
as the eyes of a stranger

that makes you want to gather up all the years
and take another good look at the map.

DOUBLE GLASS DOORS

At the airport, there's been a mix-up.
Another woman is waiting for him
at the gate, skirt melting around lean legs,
neck sloped like a doe. Heart pounding,
you dissolve into the crowd,
drive home. Later, asleep on the couch
your dreams are fluid and free
as the wedding band you threw
out the window as you drove,
arcing into goldenrod and thistle.

One afternoon he comes home,
rifles through papers, photos,
evidence of the life he would destroy
if he could, with the toss of a match
and a dash in the dark.
But I stand immovable before him,
want the faded images in black and white
that tie me to something on this earth.

Later he leaves me a note,
folded and stained with sweat, with tears,
says, "I'm in torment, let me go."

In the cool dark of the theater
you become young again,
float through a quadrille in taffeta,
ride to stippled hounds and embrace a soldier
kneeling in a swale of snow. Such a relief
simply to forget until the frames stop whirling
and your own life hits you again, head on,
like the wall of sunshine
beyond the double glass doors.

Now you drink your coffee standing at the sink,
one rubber-gloved finger
tucked into the plastic handle of your cup.
You've kept no photographs, but see him
beyond your face in the mirror.
Tonight you lead him into the garden,
straight to the blue delphiniums you loved
and remember how the two of you
watched a pair of does
crack thin ice at the edge of a pond
and wondered at the tiny axes
of their hooves.

THE DEER

By now the bones are but sloppy shorthand
for a life. The mouth is slurred with silt,
ribs protrude like long curved fingers
and the pelvis is riddled with buckshot.
The tongue that used to sing is gone
and water eddies through the teeth,
loose in their sockets.

Walking the banks of the river
that splits the land like a scar,
I scan for driftwood, river glass,
and consider my life, my ties to a place,
to a man. Married more than half my life,
the thought of leaving is almost inconceivable.
I stand twisting the end of my scarf,
looking down at the stripped apparition
anchored by the sand and sense a white tail
flashing through the trees.

A breeze ripples the surrendered water.
This creature surely knew love,
for what is running but the body in love
with its marriage to the wind?
And what these arching ribs
but the fierce embrace of sun and scent—
what these perfect hooves but anchors to the sky?

UNDER A PRAIRIE MOON

The trees stand stiff as uniformed recruits
at a mixer as the full moon's cool eye
eclipses the neighbor's pole light.
Three brothers unload hay,
speaking the blunt monosyllables
of fraternal complicity. The fourth
sits alone in his kitchen, his mind
drifting, his body echoing
the thoughts he's hidden
for so long in the silence
of blood and bone. His will accedes
to the slow burn of the body, feral
with the dark tide of blood and regret.
He stares at weathered hands, his cup
of tea and the worn linoleum
remembering her hands, cool as jazz
and her hair, long as the night ahead.

Midnight, the wind's blowing
through the stubble of crew-cut hayfields,
and the farmhouses have all gone dark.

Dawn comes gently and all rise
to face the morning: water, bread, birds
and the black wings of memory
that give no rest.

CONGO

High above, pale doomed buds emerge
amidst the flak of flying beetles.
Poisonous frogs the color of jello
clutch in mindless copulation,
secreting eggs in frothy masses
on the undersides of leaves.

Underfoot a line of giant ants
bare heavy pincer jaws,
a single file army
of the quick and the dead.
Above, meteor trails stream
off the rigid, spoked wheel of a whirling corpse.

The forest floor is a foot thick, rotting,
absorbing every bone, eyelash or bit of spittle
that falls into this living mat
of mud, piss and fiber. Am I too
part of this living food machine,
sucking death? A pearl
of loneliness lodges near my rib.
The night pulls a vine around my chest.

Dawn in the Sangre de Christos

Pale-faced, the moon eases over the canyon rim,
No wind, no birds, just the fading moonlight
bright silver on the lake.
Silver as the glint of a knife,
silver as the ping of a bell,
silver as my light in darkness.

Tonight the Leonids are lonely migrants
each a great pale lobo
as the Great Bear walks
the Sangre de Cristos til dawn.

The cool air smells of pinion and mesquite
and in the early light, the roosters begin,
loud as drunken dinner guests.
Just now, on the cusp of day
with the first light coming pink,
the cholla cacti that grab you with needles
curved like fish hooks, look soft as fur.

Even in the high desert it is springtime,
and preening in the first rays of sun nearby,
the cactus wrens are as audibly grateful
as the robins and meadowlarks in Iowa.

BAJA BEACH

All is quiet but the whispering
ebb and flow. The shoreline unspools,
a stretched canvas of crusted sand

etched with the scribbled paisley of crabs
and strewn with dreadlocked mats
of seaweed and fishing net

haloed by flies.
Under the bleeding ribbons
of contrails, the shoreline bleeds
like watercolor, wet on wet.

The diaphanous curl of the surf
ices my ankles; the tickle of geology
in fast forward erodes the sand

under my feet. By the cliffs the silence
breaks in brush stabs of rubbish:
an orange frisbee, splashes

of green glass, spill-oil congealed
on lichened boulders. Calligraphy
in disarray, pelican bones, swollen bladders

of kelp, and the persistent still life—
a split running shoe,
crushed beer cans, pop tops.

On the sequined sea a dark quiver
of frigate birds. In the sun-baked hush,
how deep the waters watching.

AMIGO

Trails of a snail's endless wandering,
the highway gleams, and mile after mile
of cragged cactus and creosote bush
permeate the air with healing after rain.

Stopping to walk in the shadowed underbelly
of slow-moving clouds we see
the discarded water bottle and empty wallet
of someone, new to this land, who huddled
in ghostly twilight dreaming
and waiting for the sky to fall.

A raven banks and turns,
its eyes full of warning.
As we drive away the earth
diffuses back to silence,
huge against the smallness
of our passing.

Late Winter

Winter persists with oddly pale skies
like an old stain of tea on damask.
I'm a bluebird in March,
back too soon and not
in the home I remembered
but in the same jacket of
skin covering bones
and the only thing that feels
like home is sleep.

I need to trim back memories of
pelicans diving into aqua,
nights of blowing stars.

Daily I make my way among
tea cups, telephone books,
early lamps, and then driving,
my mind somewhere gone from here,
I find myself at a stop sign—
snow drifting so softly that time exhales,
still as a waiting fish—
and I am seven years old watching
a paperweight of tiny deer and pines,
snow swirling thick in liquid glass.

RACCOONS

All night they soak their bones
in moonlight, chittering by the pond,
holding small bundles of fur or skin
underwater until they're limp.
They tear at chicken wire,
clawing their way into small lives
leaving only a few feathers
and a tube of scat.

Near dawn they follow the cold ripple
of a hose back to their den
in an abandoned cellar,
littered with clots of mold and broken jars.

Sometimes by day I see one sleeping
face down on the limb of an oak,
paws like tiny starfish,
a soft breeze ruffling his fur,
or find one in my live trap
covered with mud and defeat,
and take him for a drive.

When the yellow moon rises
and another night is born
in the fragrant loins of nightmare
they appear again, dark forms at dusk
humping along the hedgerows,
eyes shining with borrowed madness.

THE RATS

All summer I heard them rustling
among the eggshells, orange rinds and leaf mold
in the compost heap, seeing only perhaps
a tapered snout and quivering whiskers
before a hump of grey
slipped behind the fetid hill,
hairless whip flicking behind.
With frost on the kale
I would have thought them gone,
but today when I come to fork the pile
I startle, see the big one
backing a heel of bread into a hole,
vermilion eyes unimpeachable,
his partner reclining nearby,
lazy as a red-tailed hawk in an updraft.
Today they don't flee but wary, meet my eyes.
Leaning on the fence post I contemplate their life
among buzzing flies, rotting tomatoes
and the certainty of winter. Sighing,
I return the pitchfork to the shed.

THE DOE

When the fields are frozen and stalks are broken,
lean are those whose bellies cry in hunger.
Spring has not yet returned to the land
of the sated raven and crimson wind.
To the owl's query from the dead oak tree
in the greening night under the moon's dead eye
the hunter waits, not knowing what he'll find,
alert for footfalls, musing in his blind.

When the impresario sun gleams down,
the shadows drop into prisms of rime,
and gone is the shroud of night.
Heavy, she lifts herself from her grassy bed
with swollen udder and slowly steps
cloven into the twin streams of her breath,
all heart and light and trembling flanks
on grass sweated with frost.

When the wind pricks her guard hairs, brings his scent,
fear stabs sharp as a black locust's thorn.
She stands like a boulder yet shows through the trees.
Imagining antlers, his body freezes
and fearing to lose his mute quarry,
with hammering heart, lets fly the arrow.
Song of innocence, the moon in her heart,
In kid she's pierced, twins never to part.

When the storm prowls and the high wind keens,
the bare branches groan and the birthingwind screams,
at last he finds her but turns from the sight
of two dark forms at her feet. Retreating, he knows
that no wishing will make it undone.
Slippery and wild, she licks them dry.
The thunder's passed, and gone the fright,
the branches dripping rainbows of light.

When the blood-bright world is born next day,
cumulous foams into a pride of stallions,
their legs akimbo, enlaced with gold,
futile as dreams to her who lies dying.
Hidden in dry grass under their hooves of cotton
She's peaceful now, the hunter forgotten.
Watching the red hawk float in the sky,
her young ones against her, she closes her eyes.

THE DOG

Like reclining polar bears
smooth mounds of April snow
lounge in snowmelt catching
moonlight. I want to speed but fishtail
on new gravel, pale as chalk, scanning
for deer. At home silence greets me
and the Milky Way, losing a few
more stars. Sometime after midnight
I wake to the cacophony of relentless barking.

It's a mangy yellow dog with dusty ribs,
another rural drop-off wreaking havoc. Smelling
pheasants in the aviary, he's beaten
down a six-foot swath of garden. Yellow crocus,
the early shoots of dame's rocket, poppy
and delphinium lie in mud-raked tatters
the chicken wire drips saliva,
the pond is stirred into chocolate,
a fish curled and drying on the grass.

I subdue my body language,
issue a honeyed "come on boy," slam
the car door after his muddy frame
and wagging tail, and drive a possessed
four minutes flat into town, drop off one
filthy, confused dog at the corner of Main and D,
rationalizing, any farmer'd shoot him. I want
desperately to sleep this night, not to feel
his hope, his wild hunger and the red stream
of his life now connected to mine.

Is this even an option when we are chosen?
When the baby robin gapes up at us from the grass,
will she ever truly leave us if we walk away?

SUNFLOWERS

A few tall strangers stand aloof.
Heavy caps of pale seeds
swell dark and daily pursue
the hot medicine of
the sun's bright burn.
But despite coarsening stem
and white roots spiraling deep,
pagan wind and slash of rain
demand submission, invade
the dark and tender earth.
Blooms and stalk grown weighty,
they bend in prayer.

Raccoons break open dark umbels
to prise oily seeds delicately
from upturned chalice,
only much later pausing
to lay them aside and
return to their killing ways.

SECOND GENERATION

In the blue half light of the barn,
surrounded by curious, laughing, breathing
bodies, I rub the long, draped ears
and roman nose of my Nubian doe, then place
the flat of a hand on each sparrow-colored
flank. One side, tossing and growling
is her rumen, the other oracular,
quiet, hollow. As the last snow
mixed with rain slides down the window
I wonder if, duly seeded,
she carries life within her.
Her udder hangs loose, uneven,
deflated brown bats, but her ravening
appetite speaks of invisible life,
hot and formless, within.

There were twins, one lived,
the other died after two days,
having barely tasted the rich white honey
of life, and now spring is tossing
the air again. Three does wait for hay,
feeling the urgent quickening of their bodies.
In the orchard the grass greens invisibly,
ivory buds distend. And I, walking
the slower orbit of human generations, remain,
watching the fire of the earth
arcing, spinning with light feet
over the face of things, unconcerned
with minor extinctions or the fate
of any one small thing.

She lies on her side in the straw
haunches thrashing. For a moment she stills,
eyes glittering. A tiny white foot appears,
encased in membrane. A wave of contraction
shoots the kid out in a wet cocoon,
fighting for its first breath, fighting
to stand, to drink, to live, to do
with its few years what it will, what it must.

Under Glass

It's a sepia fall day, late afternoon
in the old print that covers the
hole in the hallway. The sky is bleached,
born of brush strokes reflecting light,
paling vestige of an artist's vision.

I am the young woman
with sun-browned skin and broad hips
gathering hay with a man's hands,
calloused and coarse, waiting
until someone needs to replay the
scene again, feel the hot
October sun on my tired back,
the sweat between my breasts.
I want you to believe in me
though I'll never know your name.

My present is fixed
as the points on a prairie star
but my past trails behind,
full as the cart mounded deep with hay
against the sluicing light.

I know how to cool fever,
birth a child. I know
the scream of the hawk and
the moan of a doe, every inch
of my husband's land
and how to pray for rain.

On the hill where my house waits,
bordered by white pines where orioles sing,
buttermilk clabbers on the sideboard
and a bowl of red currants
catches the fading sun.

(The painting is *Des Glaneuses* by Jean-Francois Millet.)

PLAYING RACHMANINOFF

Sulky twilight heavy with the emerald burden
of summer's solace. The moon comes
early, a pale cameo over sunburned fields.
In the north the wind is restless,
combs uncut grass and beards of corn,
stretching white puffs into anvils, hulking ships,
sky ponies and darkening into crusted cetaceans
booming the sky in careening decibels
amid the shatter of wind-whipped rain.

Then the cool dawn, the shining thread
of a breeze, trill of a warbler,
a woodpecker's mobile mantra
over whispering grasses. And the sun,
lifting away every trailing premonition
of ground fog, seems to offer the bliss,
not of understanding, but of absolution.

REFUGEES

In some country people are fleeing
under cover of night, in the rain,
under God's burning spotlight.

They take what they can:
furniture, chickens, a few gold bangles,
dishes perhaps, a baby wrapped in red.

They leave things: houses empty
or burning, a barrel of potatoes,
the old and unwilling, next year's seeds.

In a shed an old man is hiding.
At knife point she takes his shoes,
deliberate as the yellow moon rising.

A child's unburied body lies naked
by a shining river. Someone needed
the dress, her purple ribbon.

Wedded to destiny by the gods
of their sacrament, the red and blue
scarves they wear or don't,

their faces ebony or ivory—
these colored birds grown weary
struggle slowly in thin lines,

loss trailing them like dark hair in water.
Some cross the last invisible line, still dreamers
curled around an immutable core.

Others, intercepted, present their captors
with the singular orange gift
of their death.

PASSAMEZZO

Black as China tea it hovers
in a corner, one ebony wing
outstretched. Sometimes a few strings
sound like the faintest moan
of a woman dreaming, and when the cat
walks placidly down its perfect spine
discordant notes protest.
But when she sits to play, the adagio
of the yellow day pours in
and a few notes rise from the sleepy tangle
of clefs and bar lines to float on the river
of light. Hands reach and leap
in undulant feline play, lithe as dancers
as she rocks into the arch of phrases.
Strands of hair fall into her face
and the final passage spills like rain
that rises in tendrils from the earth,
wrapping the fields around her. Weary now,
she sees only the collapsed pale spiders
of her hands, mute carriers of song,
a glaze of perspiration on the keys.

ORANGE SUNSHINE

Four orange barrels in a velvet-lined box,
two apiece, washed down with Coke,
never mind my 100 lbs. is half yours
and I'm the one that has to drive.

Finally parked, the sky backs off
and the white noise of the motor
swirls off into the stiletto trunks of trees.

Sweltering under an oak, mouth dry as dust,
I no longer remember my name,
the stripped bare bones of my life
white and glittering. I'm old
as the limestone cliffs, need nothing,
throw comb, wallet, tangerine
lip gloss into the air, coins winking,
purse fishtailing against the blue.

The day kneels, a hot wind climbs
our backs, the sun flares violet
and we start calling in what we know.
Driving still impossible, we abandon

the car, stick out thumbs.
From a rusted Mercury
weedy smoke, a harmonic cloudburst,
two voices. I sit on your lap in the back seat,
your hands resting on the twin commas

of my sunburned hipbones, arching
over low-rider jeans, as twilight drifts
into hay fields and knee-high corn.

I comb my fingers through the cool
sheath of unflinching hair
hanging over the back of the seat
until the teeth of recollection
zip tighter, and with a tiny inswept suck
of breath, remember. We don't do that.

Now I only half remember remembering
how my hands dropped from her hair
feigning nonchalance, and discovered the heat
in my cheeks. And the relief
of walking into the cool
wafflecone air of Baskin Robbins,

then out again into the starry night.
Sucking a vanilla malted,
pinching the straw
to make it last, I smile
at the shame I walked away from.

MIDNIGHT IN MY BEDROOM

Late at night everything changes.
My oriental rug is a white-capped ocean
with crimson shoals and clouds of fish.
The gardenia's scent
floats in my bit of tropical paradise.
Nothing moves or breathes
and I'm starting to hear the voices.

I don't want milkweed in my bath tonight.
He's masquerading as a death duet.
Don't be fooled by crows at midnight.
We were three white chocolates.

OK, no more of that.
It's my world tonight and perhaps,
just this once
I can pull free from
the nacred shell of memory,
step clean, and see the earth
as washed by rain.

But it is late,
I am starting to fade
and in that nether gap
the voices continue . . .

The messengers of grace are fog bound.
My night heart, come bird song.
There they were, bananas in paradise.
It was the last job for snow canary.

Again I open my eyes to travel back,
worlds slipping like otters on a mudslide,
and I wonder, what is this wild open path
to the landscape of my secrets and lies?

They could be bubbles on a lake
from a subterranean turtle,
white egrets floating like thistle down
on the river of memory.
Or perhaps they're the seeds of my dreaming,
ready to crystallize into mirrors
that will let me see
around the corners of the maze,
if only I can remember long enough
and step between the raindrops.

LETTING GO OF YOUTH

Leading you through the trees
to the clearing I take the pins from your hair,
loosen it with my fingers and consign
it to the wind. Your skin is mica white
and your small breasts rise
as I pull off your dress of gauze
and let it fall at your feet. The line
of your neck, that tight flat belly
and fenugreek-scented arms,
your face solemn as a cat
I free to the darkness.
Obedient you slip into the moonlit
fields, wind-blown with sleep.
I keep back nothing.

Standing alone now, somehow bereft,
I want to fill myself. To wear a
dress of red velvet, to run naked
in the rain, to live without small
talk and without judgment.
To taste a lemon Popsicle,
sing hosanas, smell city streets after rain,
let the wind tangle clouds in my hair,
and feel my body's slow, sure answers
to everything.

And at the end of the day
to unbutton my courage, stretch
out that dull ache in my back and
rub sweet oil on my body in all those
places where you once were full
and pink, or downy, backlit by
red light or stars, all those tender places
where you once had been.

49

Driving Down B Street

We couldn't have missed her
there on the curb, waving and hysterical.
The lights were on, the door ajar,
and there was her lover,
just where she said he'd be,
legs protruding from the shower,
the mirror clouded up by steam.

My husband presses the blunt of his finger
into the wet skin under the jawbone,
probing for pulse. The screams
of his girlfriend rake the violet ether
under streetlights. She is ripe
with terror and his unborn child.
The medics enter in a clatter
as the freaking kitten upends a bowl of flour.
In a cloud of camphor they drag him
into the hall. A gloved hand trembles
as it empties an ampoule of amber
into the pale crook of an elbow.
A tech slaps pads onto damp blond curls.
Lungs heave to the rhythmic pump of palms.

I stand in a doorway drinking in his face,
the tangerine kitten, the chevron of medics.
But when I look away I see only the silverfish
along the baseboard, illumined
by ambulance strobe light, dark, light
until I feel the core of him disappearing,
dripping away like melting ice.

He senses the heat of her, the way her skin feels
in the morning, the soft swell of her belly,
smells muffins, hears the stop-start-sigh
of her daughter playing the cinnamon piano,
remembers the brushed pink and blue
of the summer sky like an aquarelle wash.
Then come voices people in the walls,
the silvering rise and fall of speech
and a tapping he cannot identify.
Perhaps a jaguar running in the wood
toward the sloe plum of the setting sun
into which he feels he must rise.

AND IF IT HAPPENS

If it happens that you carry
your heavy-plumed sorrow
into the sea, turn back before the swells
lift you like a lover and subsume you,
limbs curved in aqueous silence.
Remember, it is not your time.

Or when you find the world collapsed
down to your pale curled form
on the bed, sheets bruised
by wine and spilled fire, smoke
in the halo of your hair,
open the window and let the cool vector
of moonlight run down your face.
Know that the fragile monochrome body
you see in the mirror
is your home only for now.

Cup a breast in your hand,
pass a finger across your lips
and go to the garden beyond the peonies
crushed by wind, into the starlight and fireflies
and brandish the tender scalpel
of your longing. Dance abandoned,
knee deep in clover until your eyes shine
with dawn. There is no light like yours.

THE MASTER

A galactic silence
drifts over the world
during these, the Master's last days.
Each moment a button coming undone,
the jewels of the mind
exposed to float endless in time.

So many decades, obedient, we reached
for the satin muscle of truth
stretched long by invisible hands.
How we wanted to be changed,
to be absorbed. Eyes closed,
we opened the door
to silent chasms of ice,
the mists of the moon.
Everything we touched
dissolved.

Today and forever his light burns in us,
soft as a fontanel, the place
where light collects under the skin.

MEMORIAM

Standing by the wrought iron fence,
held to earth by our boots,
we lean back, take in the dark drift of the sky.
Your face is silent as the winter river,
its silver skin.

Driving back from Cloverdale
the moon flows over the highway
under the black blade of night.
In your mind's eye
you see the twelve red roses
you tossed into the earth.

In the motel room, we bury him
again and again while he sits with us
and looks on, leaving you aching,
hands full of love.

No one knows but you this harnessed longing,
how memory roams the skin
and how he held you,
tangled in the sheets and crying from a dream.

Now there's another skin inside your skin
that breathes and dreams into every corner of loneliness
like a phantom limb, his presence
floating quietly around the neighborhood.
His voice is gone, his black eyes,
but he's inside you now,
luminous in the weight of distance.

Diana

With smell of rain damp earth,
wings of snowy owl,
skin of pale velvet,
body like the spreading stain
of dark desire,
she is clothed in tattered mosses.

She is the moonlight that guides
the wheel and stream of geese,
that urges brown trout
to bouldered pools,
that inspires the flash and pivot
of running deer.

She is the dance of
granular snow on plowed fields
that frees a tuft of grey fur
from a blackberry cane,
licks the bleached scapula
lying in the grass,
and hears paw snap twig
as a low dark shadow
passes the barn.

Disappearing into the hedgerow,
face wet and teeth still pink
from the kill,
she is the breeze that lifts
the bit of feather
from his whisker
and lets it float back to earth.

GUARDIAN ANGEL

On this sleepy Monday
I must wait for her to return
and with strong hands grasp me
by my shoulders. She's floated
off this morning into the starry void
as she does on occasion
after a night of hard work
scattering the bright confetti of dreams.
Sometimes she complains
that dealing with me
is like herding tigers and flies
away from the dense jungles
of my interior.

Does she get lonely out there,
plumage heavy with the mica of star dust
knowing she must return,
tender hands ready to chip away
at the scaled shell that hides
my heart from the sun?

She's not impressed with my outrage
when I struggle in at midnight,
the car having shed a tire in the desert,
shrugs when I rail at hated winter,
or want to run the film of my life in reverse,
bring an empty spoon to my mouth
and remove it mounded with ice cream
and watch slices of cake flying
one by one back onto the plate, the candles,
all eighteen of them, smoking, then blown
into full flame by a fervent unspoken wish—
and waits for me to return
to thankfulness.

DESTINY

I saw you standing at the gate
when the tectonic plates shifted
and I was born. They could have
given me the botched elixir
of an impotent deity
but instead, you—my guardian angel?—
with your orange gloves and thrift store shades
said give her a chance
and the curtain went up.

I could have been the widow
pacing granite cliffs,
the weary saint
ladling gruel into tin cups
or one of any number
of the unnumbered,
unresurrected.

Instead you sent me home,
if home is what you'd call it;
a white clapboard house
with sudden gusts of hemp and nettles
a well full of rust
and a blight of angels under my skin.

In the barn I find a warm brown egg
ready to unfold its transparent tremolo
of destiny, but I put it into my apron
and turn my face away from you
preserving the illusion
that the next move is mine.

MY FRIEND'S DIVORCE

Driving the scalp of the hill
I peer out from window-misted haze
at summer's dissolution—
slick leaves flap heavily
and briefly join the skylitter of birds
before plastering the asphalt
under the purple cheeks
of the petulant sky.

Later my friend calls. We touch
on the weather (always the same in L.A.,
worse in Iowa), what's for dinner
and the high price of gas
before she angles for forgiveness.
Satisfied, she paints
the slow tumble of new love.

After the call I sit, twirl the phone cord
and notice the hibiscus. One flower
is beginning to fold its wrinkled chemise
around the stamen.   I leave it
though it won't last till morning.

Tomorrow, when it's just the two of us
I'll tell you more.
Tonight I'm watching
bright skirts and a wide smile collapse
around the invisible seed of the next generation.

Night-Blooming Cereus

We waited five long years
tying succulent green petiole to bamboo,
but you choose the dark swirl of this summer night
to turn back your soft mullein quilt
and rise. How awkward your single bud,
a brown bat, folded, hanging by its toes.
But your bloom . . .

Pearl white corolla curving like
an alabaster nude reaching to the sky;
we lick you up like milk.
Surprised, your stamens quiver,
shedding powdered gold,
and you blush the faintest rose
when we look again.
But the hour is well past midnight;
the reluctant moon is setting
and you are starting to pale.

Weary, we wander off—
and the clink of dishes
shreds the quiet pulse
beating at the nexus of your stamens.
Your pistils exude tiny droplets,
your ivory robes are creased and soiled.
Soon they shrivel and drop,
lying on the soil like a bat
whose echo-location has failed.
Outside an apricot dawn unfurls.

THE FIELDS ARE COMING UP

to meet the sky on tiny stems
with green or purple leaves—just two,
but soon will form a living tapestry
covering the dark scars of earth
bared by heave of frost.
As I walk I think of you these decades later,
and not without regret.
Old wounds, the wounds of winter,
are ignored but do not disappear. Dead
branches lie about on the remains
of last season's green, the shattered canes
of roses splayed in haphazard disarray.
But your brown eyes still draw mine
though you've seen many springs,
and your words lead me
along neglected paths
so that my body remembers
and learns to cry for lost parts of itself,
a face in a mirror, a hand extended, a way back.
My cat looks at me with yellow eyes,
sniffs the air. She knows I'm waiting.
Every day the sun is stronger.
Soon the brindled trees will forget
their scars in the passion of their green,
so much light breathing all around.

WAKING HOUR

Once, when the waking hour
tumbled in too early, escorted
to my rumpled bed by the insistent fever
of a dog's barking, the urgency
took me to an emerald crown
of reeds around a misted pond.
Two forms thrashed in the shallows,
slicing the water into kaleidoscopic bits
of reflected sky, splitting the air
with their primitive urgencies.
Finally a small white ball of muscled intent
rolled up the western slope,
and the coon, still standing
in the water waving his paws,
rustled off. In the quiet
my eyes quickly forgot them.
Only the slightest whiff
of astonishment hung evanescent
over dawn's cold shoulders.

LAKE KEOSAUQUA

A praying mantis hangs
on a branch over the water.
As we float on our backs
the prisms on our eyelashes
refract afternoon sunlight
into orbital moons
that reconfigure with every blink.
Our eyes issue invitations
in the language of lovers,
as pale legs frog kick,
bringing us near
or shyly sliding us away.
We are held in the body
of the lake, its seminal liquid
transmitting libidinal rift,
tired bodies and the sticky
adherence of guilt. All we know
is the slow rush of the mind
and the variegated light dappling the skin
of water under willows.
And there on a floating twig
like a ripple of memory
is a moth with furred antennae,
and wings of chameleon flames
dotted with empty eyes.
Watching it preen
with thinnest jointed limbs,
I lose myself in dream
and slap of tide. But don't be fooled.

This incandescence lasts five days
and needs only air and a floating other
to transmute its fragile genes—
something we do better on land
and call by a different name.

BEDROOM WINDOWS

They're harmless enough by day
but even on the darkest night
stars find the slightest crack
and pour in silvery minnows
that shimmer and giggle.
Some nights, from my fetal curl
in a nest of sheets, the thinnest blade
of the moon rouses me.
I hear it strike the glass with a ping,
pierce the pane, turn to butter and melt,
laughing hysterically and swelling the night
with play. Gently, insistently,
it pulls at my lashes, but the instant
I open my eyes it reverts
to its customary reserve, a wink
of chrome in the dark night sky,
its aura of unfathomable distance.

SPRING

Morning soft as feathers,
of slimmest green unfolding.
Maple seedlings covering
the ground with tender beginnings,
thrusting up bifurcated umbrellas
with the hope and abandon
of unleashed sperm.
The dandelion roots are white
as I pry them from the earth,
their leaves not bitter yet, with bloom.

My body floats on the same currents
of emergence I sense in the humming air,
the daffodil's crisp stalk,
and the purple-coated leaf buds
of the wary rose
that waited through the gyre
of winter's wild night,
bending to the clouds
and letting the wind's fury
drop deep
into her secret heart.

LAST NIGHT'S MOON

"When will we next walk together under last night's moon?"
—Tu Fu

Grey fog spills into cold valleys.
Underfoot, the black ground that ferments, eats
bones, rots flesh, preserving the seed
of a persimmon for emergence
in a freak December.

Rain pins down the skin
of the pond as we stand in wet sneakers
over a bed of bones. Beneath us
a drowned dinosaur sings in the carbon of stone,
an ancient whale groans,
shifting ever so slightly in her granite traces.
The moon stands veiled, her chemise drifting.

Mulberry trees and stalwart pines stand erect,
ivy twisting up their trunks so thick it glows,
the air redolent of dark, rich soil.
Standing mute, thoughts congeal;
buds of ice drip from bent heads
of goldenrod. The night breaks and splinters,
fractured by stars.

Home at last on a blanket of grass
our silent bodies speak, each word of skin,
a declaration.

HOME

How like this wild and rising
spring are our lives.
We grow, build fragile houses
of sticks, of words, of love,
closing our eyes only briefly
before waking once again
to dart and drowse in the world
of the scarlet tanager
and white-tailed deer,
a world of food, desire, danger
and of death.

But on occasion, one can fall
deep into the quiet of the trees,
and in that dappled world of leaves
find a silent place not reached
by footfall, its time unmeasured
by the dripping of a spring.

NIGHT VISION

Snow falls softly
and the last rosy cloud greys,
abandoning the mind's horizon.
The shoulders of hills
hunch against the cold, the field
a flat belly, punctuated by the navel
of a frozen pond. Skirting dark
clumps left by a plow,
two dogs trot a hedgerow
as the veil of night pours
over eyes that turn within.
Remembering the fire
of the invisible
I feel the body of the earth
becoming my body, my body filled
with quiet stars and snow.

ABOUT THE AUTHOR

Susie Niedermeyer is by education a classical pianist, with a degree in music performance from the University of Iowa. Her poetry has been published in journals and magazines including *The MacGuffin, Lyric Iowa, Sierra Magazine* and others; her poem "Diana" won 2nd place in a 2002 contest sponsored by the National Federation of State Poetry Societies. Her poetry also appears in *The Dryland Fish: An Anthology of Contemporary Iowa Poets* (2004) and *Leaves By Night, Flowers by Day* (2006). Susie is a nature lover and avid gardener and keeps an aviary of Chinese golden pheasants and a koi pond in her back yard.

Printed in the United States of America

www.ingramcontent.com/pod-product-compliance
Lightning Source LLC
Chambersburg PA
CBHW032029090426
42741CB00006B/781